Complete Guide to l
Puppies and

Karen Davison AMACC

Copyright 2012 Karen Davison
All rights reserved.

Table of Contents

Introduction

Positive Approach

The Importance of Cleanup

First Steps to Success

Feeding Regimes and Diet

Positive Reinforcement Training Methods

Crate Training

Advantages and Disadvantages of Neutering

Common Mistakes

Summary of Do's and Don'ts

Other Publications by Karen Davison

Introduction

This guide will give advice on all aspects of teaching your puppy or dog to be clean in the house.

With the right approach, house training is reasonably quick and easy. However if handled in the wrong way, it may not only prevent success, but can also cause a breakdown in the relationship between the owner and the dog, causing stress and anxiety in both parties.

The good news is that it is never too late to turn things around, whether you are trying to house train a new puppy, or train an older dog, a positive approach, correct clean up regimes and effective methods on how to teach elimination on command are covered in detail in the following pages. Other relevant information regarding diet, nutrition and neutering are also covered within this guide.

Above all, patience consistency and perseverance along with positive reinforcement training methods are the key to successful results.

Positive Approach

One of the most important aspects to successful house training is to avoid chastisement and punishment at all costs.

Dogs do not think in the same way as us and using punishment can cause a negative association that will be detrimental to success. For example, your puppy or dog has a house training accident and you respond by telling them off or using some other aversive punishment. Does your dog link the punishment with having an accident in the house? More likely they will form a negative association with your close proximity and the actual act itself, outside of any environmental implications.

In my experience, if accidents are handled in a negative manner, what commonly occurs is that the dog will not go to the toilet in front of the punisher as it is 'unsafe' to do so. Consequently when you take them outside, they will hold onto it, wait until they have come back in and then sneak off somewhere out of sight to produce. What usually occurs at this point is that the dog is punished more severely when it is discovered. This is not only counterproductive, but is also very damaging to the affinity of the relationship between owner and dog.

Always use a positive approach when trying to house train your dog or puppy, it will make training more reliable, will gain positive results faster and will also be more beneficial to your relationship with your dog. It is always better to actively teach them what is right, rather than attempting to teach them what is wrong.

The Importance of Cleanup

Thorough and effective clean up of accidents is vital to success. Compared to dogs, our sense of smell is virtually non existent. To get an idea of how much more refined a dog's sense of smell is, we can compare the amount of scent receptors:-

Humans - 5 Million
Terriers - 147 Million
German Shepherds - 225 Million
Bloodhounds - 300 Million

To us, cleaning up with disinfectant or floor cleaner appears to be effective, but dogs will still be able to detect the odour of urine underneath strong smelling cleaners and will consequently continue marking on top of the same spot. It is important therefore to ensure that all traces of odour are eliminated even from your dog's incredible olfactory abilities.

If your dog is inclined to repeatedly mark the same area, clean up thoroughly as outlined below; then place their crate, bed or food dish on the area to break the cycle of behaviour. Dogs will not usually soil where they eat or sleep. This is one of the advantages to crate training, which is covered in later sections.

Avoid any cleaners with ammonia as this is one of the components in urine.

Hard Floors

To effectively remove the scent you will need an enzyme cleaner and surgical spirits. Biological washing powder (not non-biological) is ideal, but you can use any enzyme cleaner from the supermarket or pet shop. Mix up a solution with warm water and thoroughly clean the area. Go over it with clean water and dry. Put some surgical spirits on either kitchen paper towel or a clean rag, and wipe over the area. This will completely remove the scent even for your dog. For older male dogs that lift the leg to urinate, do not forget to clean vertical surfaces as well. Make sure to test the application of surgical spirits in an area out of sight to check that it will not cause any damage to the surface material. Although surgical spirits will leave a very strong 'surgical' smell, it will not last long as it evaporates quickly.

Carpets and Rugs

It is better to either restrict access to areas in the house that have carpets, or remove rugs until you have achieved successful house training results, as cleaning up and removing odours is a little more involved on these types of surfaces.

Avoid using steam cleaners, as heat will bond the protein in the urine into man made fibres leaving a permanent stain and odour.

The quicker you clean up, the better. Use a good wad of kitchen paper towels or newspaper, place on the wet area and blot up the urine. Avoid rubbing action as this will only spread to a larger area. Keep replacing with clean paper towels and repeating this until the majority has been absorbed. For rugs, place a wad of paper towel underneath. The next stage is to use a solution of 50% white vinegar to 50% water. Work this solution well into the carpet fibres using a brush, this will neutralise the ammonia. Repeat the blotting process as before until most of the moisture is lifted. Scrub the area with a solution of biological washing powder and warm water, blot once again and then sprinkle with baking soda and allow to dry. Vacuum thoroughly once dry. For older stains this process may need to be repeated.

First Steps to Success

Realistic Expectations

Young puppies need time to develop the muscles that control bladder and bowel movements. This takes some time, so do not expect your puppy to be able to hold these actions reliably for any length of time until they are 4-6 months of age. This varies depending on the breed, larger dogs will take longer to develop than smaller breeds. Until such time as this is achieved you can expect to have to clean up after your puppy over night, and also if you are leaving them unattended for a length of time during the day.

Older Dogs

You may be house training an older dog, often this is because they are a rescue and may have previously been an outdoor dog. Usually training is much quicker with an adult dog, as they have much better control. Positive reinforcement, a regular feeding regime using a good quality food, proper clean up and crate training overnight (this is covered in later sections) is usually a successful approach.

If your adult dog was previously clean in the house, and begins to have accidents, the first port of call should be your vet. Urinary tract and bladder infections can cause these types of problems, and some bitches if they were neutered too early can suffer from oestrogen deficient urinary incontinence (this is discussed in later sections). These types of problems are medical issues, rather than behaviour problems, and your vet will be able to prescribe appropriate medication to alleviate the problem.

Setting up the Environment

While house training try and restrict access to a room that has a door leading to outside, preferably with a washable floor. If you know for certain that your puppy or dog has got all of their business out of the way, then it will be fairly safe to allow them access to other parts of the house if they are under strict supervision.

You can purchase puppy training pads, but my personal opinion is that they are expensive and too small to be effective. As most shops will give old newspapers out for free, this is a much more economical and more successful method. In the training area, begin by covering a very large proportion of the floor with newspaper; this should begin at the outside door, coming out into the room. Usually if there are newspapers down, puppies will go onto it to eliminate. If your puppy is missing the paper, make the area larger. Once your dog is consistently going on the paper, you can begin to gradually reduce the area by putting one less strip down. If at any time your puppy begins to miss the paper, go back a stage and increase the area of coverage again. Progress until eventually you will only have a double sheet down just inside the door, this should be done gradually over a period of time. The idea is that you will teach your dog to move towards the door, giving you a nice clear signal when they want to produce.

If you notice your puppy heading onto the paper, try and get them outside before they produce. If you missed the opportunity, always verbally praise them for going on the paper, but save the stronger reinforcement (more about this later) for when they go outside.

Remove soiled paper as soon as possible, do not forget to clean the floor thoroughly before replacing with fresh paper. If it is a dry day, you can place soiled newspaper outside and weigh down with stones to prevent it blowing away. This encourages your dog by leaving the scent in an appropriate environment.

Picking up the Signals

The more frequently you can intervene and get your dog or puppy outside, the more opportunities you will have to positively reinforce them when they do the right thing. Each success will help to make the behaviour (toileting outside) stronger

Dogs will exhibit clear behaviour cues just before they eliminate. You need to tune in to these signals, and be observant. Commonly they will stop what they are doing, put their nose to the floor and begin to sniff, this is usually an indication that they are going to urinate. Older male dogs may scent higher up along vertical surfaces, another good indicator. Pay particular attention if your dog goes to an area that they have previously soiled. Circling usually indicates that they are going to have a bowel movement.

For small puppies pick them up, try not to startle or scare them, so you can carry them out to the garden. Larger or older dogs, distract them with an excited tone, hand clapping or sound distraction like a squeaky toy, and encourage them to follow you out.

If you have missed the opportunity and your dog has already squatted, try and recall what they were doing immediately before the action, and watch for that behaviour in order to pre-empt it next time.

It is a good idea to set aside dedicated training sessions to teach them to follow you out to the garden, so that when you do need to get them out, they understand what is expected. This is achieved by associating a cue, for instance 'Lets Go', keep your tone light hearted and excited, go outside and use lots of encouragement. Reinforce them with a reward when they follow you out.

Success Breeds Success

The more you can reward your dog for going outside, the better. If behaviour is positively reinforced, it will become stronger and more likely to occur. In other words the more frequently you are successful, the more likely you are to achieve positive results. With this in mind, try and get your puppy or dog outside at regular intervals. There are certain key times when this is particularly important:-

When your dog or puppy has just woken up.
After a play session.
After eating or drinking.

Try and ensure that they have 'emptied' if leaving them unattended during the day and before settling them down for the night. Always make sure that you consistently reward them for toileting when out for walks.

Feeding Regimes and Diet

Try and have regular feeding times. Regular meals result in regular bowel movements. Dogs usually need to move their bowels 10-20 minutes after eating if fed at consistent times, but this can vary from dog to dog. It is a good idea to try and keep a record of the time after feeding that your dog eliminates, so that you can get an idea of the best times to get them outside. Young puppies will need to be fed three times a day as their stomach capacity is limited and they require a good amount of food for growth. Adult dogs generally should be fed morning and evening, this is especially important for large breeds with deep chests, two smaller meals is safer than one large feed to prevent the risk of bloat which can be life threatening if undetected. You can also reduce the risks of this problem in vulnerable breeds by using elevated food dishes.

Avoid leaving food down, if dogs are allowed to graze all day, the will defecate all day as well. If your puppy is consistently having bowel movements overnight, try and adjust your feeding times, so that they either have it done before they go to bed, or manage to hold it until morning. For instance, if the last feed time is 7pm, you could try adjusting this to 9pm. If this doesn't work try 5pm. Alternatively, you could try a later morning feed. Experiment, but if trying a new feeding time, be sure to stick to it consistently for at least a week, to allow things to settle into a routine to gauge whether it is having the desired result.

Food Quality

Another very important aspect to the amount and frequency of defecation is the quality of the food. This is relevant to dogs of all ages. If the food is high quality, it will be more digestible and produce less waste. Low quality foods usually contain a lot of cheap filler ingredients, which are less digestible creating more waste.

Protein and Amino Acids

Protein is one of the most important aspects of nutrition for dogs, this is broken down into amino acids which are the building blocks vital for health, growth and development, and the immune system.

Approximate protein requirements:-

Puppies - 28%
Adult Dogs:- 18%
Performance Dogs - 25%
Working Huskies - 35%
Lactating Bitches - 28%

The ease at which protein is broken down into its component amino acids depends on its quality and source. This is where dog food labels can be very misleading. They will list the total protein level in the food, but this does not necessarily mean that it is digestible protein. For instance, protein may be listed as meat and animal derivatives, which could be made up of items such as feathers and fur which contain very high protein, but are indigestible. Cheap food can also contain high levels of cereal proteins, which are not very digestible and lack many of the essential amino acids that are required, this causes a high volume of waste.

If the food has poor quality protein, you will need to feed your dog a much higher volume of food on a daily basis in order for them to extract the levels that they actually require. Not only do you have to feed them a larger quantity, a much higher percentage of the food will be wastage. If your dog is producing a lot of waste, it is a very good indication that the food is of low quality. Consider changing to a higher quality food.

The Benefits of Feeding a High Quality Food

In general terms, the more expensive the food is, the better the quality. The higher the quality, the less you need to feed and the same size bag will last considerably longer than cheaper food. This means that there will be very little difference in the daily feeding costs. Not only will your dog be consuming less food, they will also be able to extract more nutrition from the diet, producing far less waste. It is best to try and find a food that has a single, good quality protein source, for example chicken, lamb or fish

The other obvious advantage to feeding higher quality food is that your dog will be healthier, and will have a stronger immune system. If you change you dog's diet to a higher quality food, you will notice external indications such as a shinier healthier looking coat within a few days.

Changing the Diet

If you do decided to try a diet change, introduce it gradually over the course of a few days. Sometimes sudden diet changes can result in very loose stools or diarrhoea. Make sure that you have some of the old food still available and give 75% old food,

25% new food on day one over the course of all meals. The following day you can mix half and half, proceeding to 75% new to 25% old on day three. By day four providing you have not had any problems you should be reasonably safe to feed the new diet

Positive Reinforcement Training Methods

In this section we are going to look at how to teach your dog to go on command using positive reinforcement training. Food or treats are powerful reinforcers for behaviour and work well for most dogs. Some dogs however, prefer toys and games, so choose the reward that your dog values the most. The timing of delivery is very important. Dogs live in the moment, therefore your reaction time is crucial in order to indicate clearly that the action or behaviour is right. Even a few seconds delay in response may prevent your dog from associating the reward with the action. This is why it is so important to have a consistent method of instant response such as a marker which can be used as a rapid response to behaviour.

Markers - What they are and how to use them

A marker is usually an audible sound that can be delivered as a first and rapid response to a desired action. This gives a clear and consistent signal to your dog to let them know that what they are doing, or what they have just done, is right. Markers are used in conjunction with a reinforcer (reward) such as food, games or toys.

This method utilises Classical Conditioning, which is the pairing of two unrelated stimuli so that an association is formed between the two. The dog hears the marker, which is quickly followed by the reward (treat, toy or game. This system is a fast and effective way of teaching new behaviour.

There are two methods of marking behaviour, clicker training and verbal markers, choose the method that suits you best.

Clicker Training

Clickers are a small mechanical device that makes a distinctive 'click' sound when pressed, and can be used to mark behaviour as it occurs. The 'click' should be quickly followed by the reward (treat, toy or game).

The advantages of using clicker training:-
It is not a sound heard by your dog in any other circumstances, therefore it is a powerful and distinct marker for desirable behaviour.
It is a consistent marker, as it always sounds the same no matter who is working with the dog.
It is a calm marker delivered without emotion preventing overexcited responses.

Possible disadvantages of clicker training:-
Clickers are small and can be difficult to use for people who suffer medical conditions such as arthritis.
Clickers can be lost or misplaced.

Verbal Markers

A verbal marker is a word that you utilise specifically as a first response to indicate that what your dog is doing or has just done is right. If you choose to use a verbal marker, keep it simple and consistent. For example you could choose 'good' or 'yes'. The verbal marker should be immediately followed by the reinforcer. For example 'Yes' and reward (treat, toy or game) or 'Good' and reward.

The advantages of using verbal markers:-
You are always equipped to mark behaviour.
Hands free marking.

Possible disadvantages of verbal markers:-
Not as consistent as clickers, as the sound of the marker may vary between different handlers.

Step by Step Instruction

Reinforce the Behaviour
Taking your dog outside at regular intervals facilitates the teaching of a specific command associated with going to the toilet.

This helps to increase the possibility of success, as you can begin to get your dog to 'empty' on cue. This is particularly useful before allowing them access to the rest of the house, before settling them down for bed or before leaving them unattended during the day. Make sure you are equipped with your reinforcer (treats or toys) and your clicker if you are using one.

When you take your dog out, you must stay with them, but resist the temptation to interact with them too much. You really want them to get on with the job in hand. You will need patience as it can take some time before anything is produced. Have your clicker ready in one hand if you are using one, and have the reward in the other. As soon as they squat get ready, when they have finished, mark immediately with either your clicker or your verbal marker and follow quickly with the reward. You do not have to say anything at this stage, all we want to do is reward the behaviour we want to encourage. Stay outside for a bit longer, as sometimes puppies will urinate two or three in short succession. Each time they are successful, mark and reward. Stick to this regime for a couple of days before attempting to introduce a command for the action.

Introduce the Command

The next stage is to decide what command or cue you want to use. It doesn't matter what it is, but try and pick something simple. Some people use 'get busy' 'go potty' or 'go empty' - it is entirely up to you. Decide on a verbal cue for the behaviour and stick to it.

We want to form an association between the sound or your verbal cue and the action of going to the toilet. This is achieved by firstly introducing the command while they are still in the process. So as soon as they squat say your cue and once they finish, mark and reward. Keep to this stage for a few outdoor sessions.

The next stage is to take them outside and give the command just before they squat. Watch for the body language, you should be picking up the signals at this stage, as soon as you see the early warning signs, say your cue before your dog begins. Mark and reward when they have completed the action.

After a few repeats at this stage your dog should be associating the sound of the cue with the action so you can begin to give your command as soon as you take them out. Only say it once and just wait. You must be patient. Resist the temptation to repeat the command and give your dog time to process the information. As soon as they squat, mark and reward the behaviour. You should find that their response times improve with each success. After a few days, your dog should be eliminating on command.

Crate Training

Crates take advantage of a dogs natural denning instincts as they will usually be very reluctant to soil where they eat or sleep, which means they can be a useful tool for house training if used correctly. Crates also have the advantage of giving your puppy or dog a 'safe' area where they can retire to if they need rest, and also a safe means of confinement for transportation in the car.

Crates are available in various types and styles from plastic carry/flight boxes, framed soft material to wire collapsible cages. It must be large enough to allow your dog to stand and turn around comfortably and have space for a bed and dishes for food and water. If it is too large, your dog may soil inside the crate if there is too much space in front of their bed. so choose the size carefully. You should never use a crate as a punishment area or allow children to tease dogs when they are in their crate, as your dog should associate this area with comfort and safety. As a safety precaution, it is advisable to remove collars and name tags as they have the potential to get caught which could result in a choking or strangulation hazard.

How in Introduce a Crate Correctly.

Whether you are introducing a crate to a puppy, juvenile or an adult, never force your dog into the crate. It is far better for them to explore it voluntarily, and decide for themselves that it is a good place to be. Introduction can take days or weeks depending on the dog. The most important thing is to work in gradual stages. Place some nice comfortable bedding into it, avoid using newspaper, as this is associated with toileting. Begin by throwing in a few treats and their favourite toys, leave it open and allow your dog to investigate in their own time so that your dog will associated going into his crate as a rewarding experience. Do this regularly until your dog is happily going in and out of their crate to explore what interesting items may be on offer. You can then begin to put their food inside the crate at meal times, whilst leaving it open. Often if you leave the crate door open your dog may begin to take themselves off into the crate for a nap. Once they are comfortable with the crate, you can begin to close the door for short periods of time when they are eating or sleeping. Gradually increase the time they are in their crate in small increments.

Location of the Crate

One of the advantages of crates is that they are movable; so you can place your dog's crate near you for company when watching TV or reading the newspaper. This allows you to notice the moment your puppy wakes up from a nap, so that you can then get them outside immediately.

Duration of Closed Crates

While crates can be a very useful tool, they can be open to abuse and dogs should never be shut into crates for long periods of time. Guidelines for maximum crate use as follows:-

Puppies up to 10 weeks 30 mins – 1 hour
Puppies 11-14 weeks – 1-2 hours
Puppies 15-20 weeks – 3-4 hours
Adult dogs - Overnight

If you shut your dog or puppy in for longer than they are able to 'hold it', inevitably you are going to have soiling in their crate, this will be detrimental to your house training efforts, and could put training back by a few weeks. It is advisable to ensure that your dog or puppy has 'emptied' before you close them into their crate. Puppies should not be shut in overnight until they have developed adequate muscle control. Leave the door open making sure that the area immediately outside of their crate is covered in newspaper.

Advantages and Disadvantages of Neutering

There are so many different schools of thought in connection to neutering. It can be confusing for owners to make an informed decision as to the right age to get their dog neutered, or indeed whether they should get them neutered at all. The reason that I have included neutering in this publication is that it does have some implications in connection with the subject covered in this guide.

In general terms I would be an advocate of neutering. It has many health and behavioural benefits, as well as helping to reduce the amount of unwanted dogs destroyed every year. However, it is important to consider the timing of such procedures in order to reap the maximum benefit, and reduce the risk of detrimental health problems, which can occur if neutering is carried out too early.

Males

Castrated males are less likely to be aggressive or be aggressed upon by other male dogs, and will be less likely to roam. It also removes the risk of testicular cancer.

Unneutered mature male dogs will scent mark, which can contribute to house training problems. This behaviour is not connected to the need to empty their bladder; rather, they will leave small splashes of urine in strategic areas to mark territory, That is why males 'cock' their leg, so that the urine they leave is at nose level for other dogs, and will not be missed. This behaviour begins when they reach sexual maturity which will vary from dog to dog. Puppies and juvenile males squat until such time as their testosterone levels begin to rise.

Optimal Time to Neuter Male Dogs

Large breeds mature slower than small dogs, and even within the same breed development times will vary between individuals. This is why it is inadvisable to specify that males should be neutered at a specific age. The optimum time for neutering of males is when they first begin to tentatively lift their leg when urinating. This shows that the particular dog is beginning to sexually mature. If neutering occurs at this time it will reap the maximum benefits, prevent the development of scent marking behaviour, and other testosterone related issues, such as inter dog aggression and roaming.

Implications of Neutering Too Early

Physical – Males that are castrated before reaching maturity often grow taller than they should, as the lack of dihydrotestosterone fails to signal the cessation of bone growth at the normal time. This can result in dogs that are too long in the leg and occasionally can cause disproportionate growth between the fore and hind legs, putting pressure on the skeletal structure, in particular the hips and spine.

There also seems to be some evidence of a link between osteosarcoma (bone cancer) and prepubescent castration in male dogs.

Behavioural – From a behavioural perspective, my own observations over the course of many years suggest that neutering males before they mature has the effect of 'locking' dogs into a juvenile psychological state. This can result in dogs that do not develop emotional maturity, remain 'giddy' and retain a shorter attention span.

Neutering Older Dogs

Behavioural benefits of neutering, reduce if castration is carried out when dogs are well in to maturity. In the case of scent marking for example, although testosterone was the driving force behind the original behaviour, it will soon become normal behaviour for the dog. Consequently if the behaviour has become well established, removal of testosterone due to castration may have little or no effect. Although there may be other benefits of later neutering, scent marking may not necessarily improve following the procedure.

Bitches

In bitches, spaying reduces the risk of mammary cancer as well as removing the risk of pyometra (life threatening womb infection which can proceed a season). Spaying stops the bitch coming into season, which cuts out all the inconvenience of visiting male dogs and having to keep the bitch under tight control to prevent accidental mating. Some female dogs can suffer from temperament changes during oestrogen and progesterone production. As this only occurs during and immediately after a season, spaying can have a positive stabilising effect.

Implications of Spaying Too Early

As with male dogs, it is inadvisable to neuter females before they are sexually mature. The consequence of prepubescent spaying can be a life time of urinary incontinence, as the lack of oestrogen has a direct influence on the development of the sphincter muscles. The only way to ensure that bitches have reached sexual maturity is to allow them to have their first season. The age at which this occurs again varies from breed to breed and bitch to bitch. Usually between the ages of 7 to 10 months, but larger breeds may be much later. Once the bitch has finished her season, you should leave it at least 10 weeks before considering surgery, as bitches produce progesterone for 9 weeks following a season, and should not be spayed during hormone production as a sudden cut off can cause long term behavioural complications.

My best advice to owners is to read as much on the subject of neutering as possible, talk to your vet, and make the decision that you feel is right for your own dog.

Common Mistakes

Never leave the outside door open. Often owners think that if they leave the door ajar, the dog will voluntarily go out to go to the toilet. This is not usually the case. If the door is open all the time, there is no difference to the dog between inside and outside, it is all part of the same space. We want them to disassociate between the two.

Leaving newspaper down for too long. Once you are starting to get reliable results and your puppy is showing signs of being able to hold it for a reasonable amount of time, stop putting paper down in the house if you are in attendance. This is only giving permission for them to continue to eliminate in the house. You can begin by just putting paper down over night, or if you are leaving them for a long period of time during the day. Stop putting paper down once your puppy is able to hold it over night,. Don't worry if you get the odd accident.

Summary of Do's and Don'ts

DO:-

Clean up accidents as soon as possible using an effective cleaning regime.

Take your dog outside at regular intervals, especially after napping, playing or eating, and before leaving them during the day, or settling them down for the night.

Watch out for body language signals so you can get them outside before they produce.

Always use a positive approach to training.

Always verbally praise if your dog eliminates on the newspaper.

Strongly reinforce by giving an extra reward if they go outside, or when out for walks.

Feed at regular times each day, using a good quality food.

DO NOT:-

Punish your dog for house training accidents. No shouting, smacking or nose rubbing.

Use steam cleaners on carpets, or use any cleaning products that contain ammonia.

Leave the outside door ajar for long periods of time.

Continue to leave paper down in the house once your puppy has developed good control.

Leave food down all the time so the dog can graze all day.

About the Author

"Being a professional dog trainer is such a rewarding occupation. There is nothing better than working with people to help them gain control, build strong bonds and develop a mutually enjoyable relationship with their companions."
Karen

Karen Davison is an Associate Member of the Animal Care College, Ascot, England; is passionate about dogs, their welfare and building positive relationships between dogs and their owners.

Karen holds academic qualifications in Canine Psychology, Advanced Wolf Behaviour and Ecology, Advanced Canine Behaviour Psychology and Training, and Dog Agility Instruction, and has been working as a professional dog trainer and veterinary referral behaviourist since 2001. An important part of her work has been not only training dogs and improving their quality of life, but also working to educate their human companions.

Karen has also been involved in dog rescue, rehabilitation and re-homing for many years in Co Kerry, Ireland, where she lives with her husband, two daughters and their own six rescue dogs.

Other Publications by Karen Davison

The Perfect Companion – Understanding, Training and Bonding with Your Dog!

Paperback Edition:-
ISBN-10: 1475235291
ISBN-13: 978-1475235296
Kindle Edition
ASIN-B0083J6YZ0
Ebook Edition:-
ISBN- 9781476361932

A must have book for all pet dog owners! Positive reinforcement training techniques are discussed and explained, with step by step instructions on how to teach basic behaviour are covered in detail. It also includes a comprehensive section on the importance and methods of increasing mental stimulation as well as problem solving. Some aspects of canine psychology, including the newest and most up to date concepts in the field with regard to pack rule theory, are explored. The author explains that attempting to dominate our dogs is detrimental to the affinity of our relationship with them. Treating our pets with respect, consistency and compassion, results in dogs that are well behaved, confident and happy, allowing us to build a strong and mutually enjoyable relationship.

Printed in Great Britain
by Amazon.co.uk, Ltd.,
Marston Gate.